BUS OPERATORS 1970
Midlands and Wales
Gavin Booth

Ian Allan
PUBLISHING

Contents

Front cover: Potteries Motor Traction was one of the most charismatic operators in the Midlands, running a mixed fleet on urban and rural routes. This is a 1957 Albion Aberdonian MR11L with 44-seat Willowbrook body at Stone.
Tony Moyes

Back cover, upper: Rhondda Transport was one of several operators in the newly-created National Bus Company serving South Wales in 1970. This 1961 AEC Regent V with Metro-Cammell 70-seat forward entrance body is seen at Treorchy in September 1970.
Mark Page

Back cover, lower: The creation of West Midlands PTE in 1969 had a major impact on transport services in that conurbation. The PTE's inherited bus fleet included a number of fairly elderly Birmingham City Transport standard types, like this 1953 Daimler CVG6 with 55-seat Crossley bodywork, seen at Pheasey in 1971.
Mark Page

Previous page: Municipal transport was alive and well throughout the area in 1970, although four undertakings had recently disappeared into the new West Midlands PTE. Symbolising old-fashioned municipal pride is this 1966 Leyland Titan PD3/4 with East Lancs 73-seat body from the Merthyr Tydfil fleet.
Geoff Lumb

This page: Leicester City Transport was one of the first customers outside the state-owned sector to buy Bristol/ECW buses when these came back on to the open market. This is a 1967 RESL6G with 42-seat body.
T W Moore

Facing page: Crosville still had more than 1,000 buses in 1970 covering an area that stretched from north-west England across much of North Wales. This 1964 Bristol FLF6B wears the double-deck coach livery and has seats for just 55 passengers.
Edward Shirras

First published 2006

ISBN (10) 0 7110 3035 9
ISBN (13) 978 0 7110 3035 0

© Ian Allan Publishing Ltd 2006

Design by Hieroglyph

Published by Ian Allan Publishing

An imprint of Ian Allan Publishing Ltd, Hersham, Surrey KT12 4RG

Printed by Ian Allan Printing Ltd, Hersham, Surrey KT12 4RG

Code: 0610/C

Visit the Ian Allan Publishing website at www.ianallanpublishing.com

Introduction

A great deal was happening in the Midlands and Wales in 1970, and more changes would follow in 1971 as the new National Bus Company started to rationalise its diverse and sometimes overlapping companies.

With two of England's biggest bus operators, Midland Red and West Midlands PTE, the still-mighty Crosville, the country's second largest independent operator, Barton Transport, plus a significant number of NBC and municipal companies to cover in this book, operating a great variety of vehicle types, it has not been possible in 80 pages to provide a proper coverage of independent operators – and there were many of these, particularly in the more rural parts of Wales and in Derbyshire and Staffordshire. To compensate we have provided a small selection of photos of independents in each of the chapters, concentrating on the firms that will be better-known to readers of this book.

The formation of West Midlands PTE in 1969 had a major impact on transport in that heavily-populated area, and would lead to a dramatic reduction of the powerful Midland Red empire within a few years.

The buses operated in Wales and The Midlands were sometimes simply standard-issue Tilling or BET group fare, but there were enough operators with enough muscle to develop their own individual styles – like Barton, Birmingham, Nottingham and Walsall – and of course there was Midland Red's huge fleet of own-make BMMO vehicles, incorporating many advanced features. So there is no shortage of vehicle variety in this book and I am grateful to the photographers who provided material, notably Geoff Lumb and Mark Page who both went to great lengths to identify and select photos.

Apart from the changes that followed the setting up of West Midlands PTE, Wales and The Midlands seemed very settled in 1970. The first day of 1971 heralded the great reorganisation of NBC's interests in South Wales, as well as the absorption of Stratford Blue into the parent Midland Red company. After that, the changes would come thick and fast. ∎

Gavin Booth
Edinburgh

Midlands and Wales Snapshot

From the transport point of view the area covered by this book offers a fascinating mix of bus operators, ranging from some of the very largest in the UK to tiny Urban District Council and independent fleets. All of the sectors are represented – a newly-created Passenger Transport Executive (West Midlands PTE); territorial companies newly under the control of the National Bus Company whose roots were not only in the former 'big two', BET and Tilling, but were also once in smaller groupings like Balfour Beatty and Red & White; municipal operators from Nottingham with over 400 buses, Cardiff, Coventry and Leicester, which each had over 200 buses, to tiny Bedwas & Machen UDC with just six buses; and of course there were the independent bus operators, ranging from Barton Transport, the biggest with 330 vehicles, down to local operators with fleet totals in single figures.

In topographical terms, Wales and the Midlands covers everything from the flatlands of Lincolnshire through the hills of the East Midlands across to the mountains of North Wales. The area includes what were then important coal-mining areas like South Wales and the East Midlands, the concentration of heavy industry in the West Midlands that included bus and car building, and the importance of farming right across the area.

There are traditional seaside resorts like Colwyn Bay, Llandudno, Rhyl and Skegness, and significant tourist attractions like Snowdonia, the Peak District, the Wye Valley, and historic centres like Lincoln, Oxford, Stratford-upon-Avon and Worcester.

History created the situation where there were often large numbers of bus operators serving the urban areas. For example, in 1970 there were still eight NBC companies and nine municipal operators serving the fairly concentrated South Wales area. But there were also the giants – the new 2,000-plus vehicle West Midlands PTE, and 1,760-strong Midland Red covering a vast area, and 1,045-strong Crosville, also covering a vast area, but a very different one from Midland Red's.

Although Crosville had busy urban services in Cheshire and on Merseyside, outside the scope of this book, its North Wales operations were providing essential transport for many small communities. Midland Red, on the other hand, provided intensive urban services around Birmingham and the Black Country, as well as networks around cities like Leicester and in many significant market towns throughout its area.

A lot of the structure of the bus industry in the Midlands and Wales would change over the two decades after 1970, often in quite unexpected ways. The local government reorganisation of 1974 reduced the number of municipal operators, and Midland Red's dramatic sale of its West Midlands operations to West Midlands PTE and the splitting of Crosville prior to privatisation changed the map significantly. The sad demise of the National Welsh empire was another shock.

Although nobody could have anticipated the changes, the bus operator map has changed spectacularly since 1970, with vast areas now dominated by Arriva, First and Stagecoach, operators that would not emerge for at least ten years. There are still reassuringly familiar names around – Cardiff, Newport and Nottingham still have municipal buses, and Trent and Barton survive – though now under common management – and City of Oxford still runs buses in that city. But the buses, and sometimes the colours they wear, will certainly have changed. ∎

Midland Red was an important force over a wide part of the Midlands, although in 1970 it built its last BMMO vehicles and would buy only proprietary types. Two BMMO-built buses at Loughborough in 1972 are, left, a 1960 D9 with BMMO) 72-seat body and a 1965 S17 with BMMO/Plaxton 52-seat body.
Mark Page

Setting the scene

The British bus industry was not at its most robust in 1970, with costs rising and passenger numbers falling, but at least something was being done about it.

The industry had been so busy managing decline that it had lost sight of the need to move forward. The Labour Government had decided that something had to be done, and in the late 1960s introduced a package of major changes that were designed to stem the losses by restructuring large sections of the industry and offering incentives to encourage bus operators to make economies by moving to driver-only operation.

The restructuring affected the state-owned and municipal sectors. Two in every three vehicles in the UK's total bus and coach parc were in public ownership; take hire and tour coaches out of the equation and the figure is closer to nine in ten. This had not been the case during most of the 1960s but it took the BET Group's decision to sell its UK bus interests to the state-owned Transport Holding Company to set in motion the creation of a new giant bus group, which was set up in 1969 as the National Bus Company. This combined the Tilling and BET bus companies in England and Wales – some 20,000 buses – and it had even been thought that the state-owned Scottish Bus Group could be included in a truly national company, but the rumblings of nationalism and devolution persuaded Westminster that a new Scottish body, the Scottish Transport Group, would assume responsibility for the buses and west coast ferries north of the border.

The changes of 1969 were certainly felt in Wales and the Midlands, with the bringing together of different cultures under new giant umbrellas. The creation of NBC made for some strange bedfellows as neighbouring Tilling and BET companies found themselves now in the same ownership. It was no real problem for the Crosvilles and Midland Reds, but in areas like the East Midlands and South Wales, smaller companies from both camps were no doubt wondering if they could all survive. As we would find out, there would shortly be moves to tidy up the situation.

During the 1960s bus design had moved on and the traditional front-engined double-deckers and underfloor-engined single-deckers were being joined by increasing quantities of rear-engined buses. For double-deckers this meant that driver-only operation became a real possibility, and the Government helped things along by offering Bus Grants towards the purchase of new buses suitable for what was still called one-man operation. With the Government picking up the bill for 25 per cent, and soon 50 per cent, of the cost of new buses, it was little surprise that bus operators throughout the country rushed to place orders.

Part of the problem here was that there were few manufacturers left in Britain to handle the orders, Or rather, there were still nominally several major manufacturers, but most of them were owned by British Leyland. So AEC, Bristol, Daimler, Guy and of course Leyland itself, were essentially one giant firm building bus chassis at various plants throughout Britain. Not only that, British Leyland also owned three of the biggest bus body builders – Eastern Coach Works (ECW), Park Royal and Roe.

This allowed British Leyland to control and manipulate the bus market, much to the dismay of some significant operators who wanted to have real choice available. You could buy the lighter-weight Bedford and Ford chassis, as indeed many operators did, and Seddon would make its mark with its rear-engined RU model, and although Dennis had temporarily dropped off the radar, companies like DAF, Scania and Volvo were busily making their plans to export chassis to Britain. Scania had already formed a liaison with MCW to produce a single-deck citybus for the UK market, the Metro-Scania, and this sold to operators who were concerned about the British Leyland monopoly.

The former Balfour Beatty companies, Mansfield District, Midland General and Notts & Derby, were not typical Tilling Group fleets, not least because of their liveries. A reminder that the Midlands boasts some attractive countryside is provided by this Derbyshire view of a 1956 Bristol LS6G with 43-seat ECW body from the Midland General fleet.
Geoff Lumb

A particular concern for UK bodybuilders was the Leyland National, the integral single-deck citybus that was launched in 1970 and which would dominate single-deck bus sales for the next decade. To boost National sales Leyland would drop its existing rear-engined single-deck range, the AEC Swift, Bristol RE, Daimler Roadliner and Leyland Panther, all types that had been bodied by builders like Alexander, East Lancs, Marshall, MCW, Northern Counties and Willowbrook, and while some like Alexander, East Lancs, MCW and Northern Counties were principally double-deck builders, all of them must have felt very vulnerable. As we would see, Marshall and Willowbrook would become more involved in double-deckers.

Then of course there was Midland Red, building its own range of buses and coaches in-house for more than 40 years, and although it had once built buses for other companies, since the end of World War 2 its entire production was for its own use. It had pioneered some very advanced designs, and while other large operators could buy vehicles tailored specifically to their own needs, the Midland Red situation was unique. The reality, though, was that this situation could not continue. From time to time it had bought buses from commercial builders, but this began in earnest in the early 1960s with batches of Leyland Leopard single-deckers and Daimler Fleetline double-deckers, and the last BMMO type, an S23 single-decker, was completed in 1970.

All of the changes to the structure of the British bus industry would help buy it some time. After the initial reshuffling, National Bus simplified its territorial map and started to buy large batches of largely standardised buses. The municipal sector would be affected by local government changes in the mid-1970s, and the whole industry would be thrown up in the air with the regulatory and ownership changes of the 1980s. But that was at least a decade away in 1970, so the industry had a bit of time to get its house in order – which, as things turned out, was just as well. ∎

Models like the Bristol RE would be discontinued in the early 1970s to allow Leyland's new National to survive. This is a Crosville RESL6G with 42-seat ECW dual-purpose body, in Chester when new in 1967.
R L Wilson

Wales

In the previous book in this series, covering South-West and Central England, the old Ian Allan 'ABC' pocket books in the British Bus Fleets series came in useful when I was subdividing the area into chapters. This time it's not so easy. Yes, there was a South Wales ABC, but Colwyn Bay's and Llandudno's buses were lumped in to the North Western Area book, and Crosville was one of the select few operators to merit its own ABC. Midland Red and Birmingham City belonged to that same band, of course, while at the fringes, City of Oxford was counted as 'South Central' and Lincolnshire Road Car was in 'East Anglia'.

At least Wales is easy to define, with concentrations of bus operation along the north coast, much of it in Crosville hands, and the sometimes bewildering mass of state-owned, municipal and independent operators in South Wales. Crosville's tentacles stretched down the west coast of Wales to Aberystwyth and beyond, but there was nothing on the same scale in Mid Wales.

Starting in the north, although Crosville is readily associated with its Welsh operations, it was of course an English company – just – based in Chester. Its operating area in England radiated out from Chester towards the Wirral Peninsula, Liverpool and Warrington, with services to places like Crewe and Nantwich in Cheshire, and to Oswestry on the Welsh border.

Founded in 1906 as a motorcar assembler, Crosville (the name comes from its founders, Crosland Taylor and Georges Ville) started in bus operation in 1911 from its Chester base. It expanded after World War 1 and was quickly bought up by the LMS railway company in 1929, to be renamed LMS (Crosville). A year later it was reformed under BAT-Tilling control as Crosville Motor Services Ltd, passing in 1942 to Tilling, and into state ownership in 1948.

Like so many other territorial companies it gained territory by expansion in the 1920s and 1930s, gradually increasing its presence in North Wales and beyond.

The original Crosville had been a staunch Leyland fan but when it passed into Tilling's hands it moved quickly on to the Bristol/ECW combination.

By the 1960s Crosville was listing around 1,000 bus services, though many were very infrequent or were special works services. In Wales there were concentrations of services in and around towns like Aberystwyth, Bangor, Caernarvon (as it was then spelt), Denbigh, Holyhead, Llandudno, Mold, Pwllheli, Rhyl, and Wrexham, with depots in most of these places, and enquiry offices and bus stations at these and other Welsh towns.

Above: The lightweight Bristol SC4LK chassis was ideal for many of Crosville's lightly-loaded rural routes, and this 1957 example with ECW 35-seat body, is at Talywern in 1970 on its route from Machynlleth.
Tony Moyes

Left: The Bristol LH provided Crosville with a newer generation of smaller buses, and this LH6P with ECW 45-seat body, new in 1970, is rounding a hairpin bend on its journey from Clarach to Aberystwyth.
Tony Moyes

Above: The Crosville fleet was largely composed of Eastern Coach Works-bodied Bristols for many years. This is a 53-seat ECW-bodied RELL6G loading at Holyhead.
Mark Page

Left: A peaceful 1969 Aberystwyth view showing a 1957 Bristol Lodekka LD6B with 60-seat ECW body. The Crosville fleetnumbering system used codes to signify chassis and engine types, so DLB909 was a Double-deck Lodekka Bristol engine. The later FS type Lodekka with Gardner engine was type DFG.
Tony Moyes

Opposite top: Crosville served many rural areas in North Wales. This is Llanafan Church, south of Aberystwyth, with a 1960 Bristol MW6G with 41-seat ECW body, seen in 1969.
Tony Moyes

Opposite centre: A 1962 Western Welsh Leyland Atlantean PDR1/1 with semi-lowheight Weymann 70-seat body leaves Newport bus station; it was one of 66 similar buses bought in 1960-62.
Geoff Lumb

Opposite below: South Wales Transport (SWT) was very much an AEC fleet for many years, but Leylands joined the fleet following the 1962 transfer of the James, Ammanford business. This 1963 Leyland Leopard PSU3/2R with Marshall 53-seat body was one of three ordered by James but delivered to South Wales. It is at Llanelli station in 1969.
Mark Page

All but 16 of Crosville's 1970 fleet of 1,086 buses (523 double-deck, 407 single-deck, 115 coaches) were Bristols with ECW bodies; the others were Bedford and Commer coaches. Crosville had operated virtually a full house of Bristol/ECW products, and the oldest examples still in the fleet in 1970 were 1950-delivered LL5G and LL6B 39-seat buses; the oldest double-deckers were early LD type Lodekkas, including a pre-production example. During the 1950s Crosville bought more LDs, as well as examples of the underfloor-engined LS and MW types, in both bus and coach form. The simple SC4LK rural bus was bought in substantial numbers – 79 between 1957 and 1961 – and these helped to keep many deep rural services going. There were sizeable deliveries of the flat-floor Lodekka in FS, FSF and FLF form. Some of these, like earlier LD types, were coach-seated, painted in cream with black relief rather than in Crosville's traditional Tilling green/cream; there were also open-top Lodekkas.

From 1964 Crosville bought Bristol's rear-engined RE type, first in RELH coach form, and then as RELL buses, some with two doors. The shorter RESL was bought in 1969. For private hire and excursion work, the company departed from its Bristol/ECW purchasing pattern in 1967/69 and bought Bedford VAM5 coaches with Duple and Plaxton bodies. Another Bristol/ECW type to join the fleet from 1969 was the LH, the mid-sized underfloor-engined single-decker.

After 1970 the Crosville fleet would take on a more varied appearance. With RE deliveries slow as Bristol/ECW struggled to keep up with NBC's orders, Crosville was the recipient of 100 Seddon Pennine RU buses with Pennine bodies; these were delivered in 1971/72. Then in 1972, following the acquisition by Selnec PTE of a large part of NBC's North Western company, Crosville was allocated the remaining parts of North Western territory, including depots at Macclesfield and Northwich and a mixed bag of over 100 buses, including such decidedly non-Bristol/ECW products as Willowbrook-bodied AEC Reliances and Alexander-bodied Daimler Fleetlines.

Also in 1972 Crosville would expand to the south, acquiring services in West Wales from its NBC brother, Western Welsh, along with some Leyland Tiger Cubs.

Although it operated as far west as any of the NBC South Wales companies, Western Welsh really

Left: In Wrexham bus station in July 1970 on service to Mold, a newly-delivered Bristol RELL6G with 53-seat ECW body.
J G Carroll

Below: Thousands of bus photographs have been taken over the years at Cardiff bus station, and this is a Western Welsh Leyland Titan PD2A/27 with 65-seat Weymann forward entrance bodywork, one of 21 delivered in 1963.
G Mead

engined AEC and Leyland double-deckers, returning to Atlanteans in 1969.

Western Welsh buses were red/cream, but its small coach fleet and its semi-coaches were painted blue/ivory.

Just as the Western Welsh name may not have been geographically correct, the company called South Wales Transport operated intensive services in the area around Swansea. Another red/cream BET company, it was formed in 1914 to operate feeder bus services from BET's Swansea trams. The bus company gradually increased its operating area, partly through important acquisitions like the Llanelly trolleybus system and bus operator, James of Ammanford, also a BET fleet.

Based in Swansea, South Wales was notable for its fondness for AEC chassis; the fleet was 100 per cent AEC at the time it acquired the 100 per cent Leyland fleet of James. The South Wales AECs were largely Reliance single-deckers and Regent double-deckers, with a few Bridgemasters and Renowns for good measure. The Bridgemaster was quite popular in

had its heart much further east, in the Cardiff area. The Western Welsh name was adopted in 1929 when South Wales Commercial Motors bought the Great Western Railway's bus services in South Wales and Monmouthshire. The company grew naturally and by acquisition, and its operating area was larger than any of its fellow NBC companies, stretching as far west as St David's and right across to the English border on the east. There was, of course, inevitable overlap with the other NBC companies, although each one had its particular patch.

As a former BET fleet, Western Welsh had a more mixed fleet than Crosville. Of the 569 buses in the fleet in 1970 (177 double-deck, 280 single-deck buses, 58 semi-coaches, 54 coaches), more than four in every five were Leylands, and most of the others were AECs, with a small fleet of Albion Nimbus midibuses as well. Bodywork was by a range of builders, but Weymann and Park Royal dominated.

Western Welsh built up a sizeable fleet of over 300 Leyland Tiger Cubs between 1953 and 1968 together with 40 of the similar, but integrally-built, Olympian.

Early examples of Leyland's rear-engined Atlantean were bought in 1960-62, but the company then turned back to front-

South Wales, as Cardiff Corporation and Western Welsh also had examples. The 1970 South Wales fleet comprised 319 buses and coaches (186 double-deck, 109 single-deck, 24 coaches). Its newest vehicles in 1970 were AEC Reliances with Marshall bus and Duple and Plaxton coach bodies; its newest double-deckers were 1967 Willowbrook-bodied AEC Regent Vs.

South Wales Transport buses replaced the Swansea trams in 1937 and so became the town's local service operator. It also owned the lease on the famous Swansea & Mumbles Railway, and buses replaced the trams in 1960.

Other South Wales services covered points on the coast and inland to Ammanford, Pontardawe and Llandilo.

Another NBC operator in the Swansea area was United Welsh, a former Tilling company that had started out in 1938 to collect together several smaller companies acquired by the Red & White group. It passed with this group into Tilling ownership in 1950. United Welsh operated in broadly the same territory as South Wales Transport, on licences that had been taken over by Red & White from smaller operators in the area. Its head office was in Swansea and its buses were painted Tilling red/cream.

At first under Tilling ownership the United Welsh fleet had

reflected Red & White's preferences, notably Guys and Albions, but eventually the Bristol/ECW combination crept into the fleet. The 1970 fleet of 154 vehicles (77 double-deck, 61 single-deck, 16 coaches) was mainly of Bristol/ECW manufacture, other than Duple-bodied Bedford coaches, and the newest deliveries were RELL6G buses.

Within the same area was Thomas Bros (Port Talbot) Ltd, formed in 1951 by BET after it acquired four local operators in the heavily industrialised Port Talbot area. The small fleet, 45 single-deckers and seven coaches in 1970, was pretty much standard BET fare – AECs and Leylands with BET-style bodies.

Another smaller operator was the grandly-named Jones Omnibus Service Ltd of Aberbeeg, in Ebbw Vale, north of Cardiff. It had been in business since 1921, but in 1969 had decided to sell out to the new National Bus Company, which placed it under the control of Red & White. In 1970 Jones had 22 single-deck buses and 18 coaches, mainly of AEC and Leyland manufacture.

Two other NBC companies operated in South Wales – Rhondda and Red & White. Rhondda Transport grew from a tramway operation in the Rhondda area, running trams and buses from 1920 and buses only from 1934. In 1970 the company, based at Porth, operated 164 buses (96 double-deck, 53 single-deck, 15 coaches). The latest deliveries in 1970 were Leyland Atlantean/Northern Counties double-deckers and a Leopard coach.

Red & White had an interesting history. Red & White Services Ltd was set up in 1930 to consolidate several businesses that were in the same ownership. Although based in Wales, Red & White continued to build up an empire that included bus companies in Basingstoke, Cheltenham, Gloucester and Newbury. By the early postwar years Red & White had grown to become the largest company operation outside the BET, Tilling and Scottish groups, and it voluntarily sold its British bus business to the British Transport Commission in 1950. The Red & White empire was broken up among other Tilling fleets, and the remaining portions in Wales were the United Welsh company, already mentioned, and Red & White itself, based in Chepstow.

Red & White's operations stretched as far as Swansea in the west and

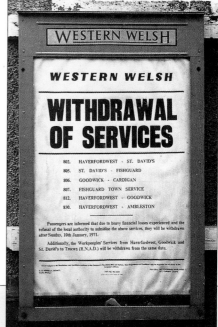

Above: **Although Western Welsh tended to favour Leylands, it also bought AECs, often for coach and dual-purpose duties. This is one of 12 Reliance 2MU3RA with Willowbrook 41-seat bodies bought in 1961 for longer-distance trips, but demoted to bus work when photographed.**
Edward Shirras

Right: **Western Welsh built up a massive fleet of Leyland Tiger Cub buses between 1953 and 1965, most with 44-seat Weymann bodies like this 1956 PSUC1/1 on the last day of operation of the St David's-Fishguard service, in January 1971. This was one of several routes in the western part of its area abandoned at that time.**
Tony Moyes

Gloucester in the east, with links into the South Wales valleys and outside Wales to Hereford and Ross-on-Wye. Its 1970 fleet comprised 393 buses and coaches (72 double-deck, 244 single-deck, 60 coaches), all Bristol/ECW products – there had been a major move away from the once-favoured Albion products following the BTC acquisition. The newest deliveries in 1970 were Bristol RE buses and coaches.

There was one other NBC fleet in South Wales, Neath & Cardiff Luxury Coaches Ltd. This former BET company differed from its fellow NBC fleets in that it only operated coaches, specifically between Swansea and Cardiff. In 1970 the brown/red-liveried coaches, known locally as 'Brown Bombers', were AECs with bodies by a range of coachbuilders.

Wales still boasted 11 municipal bus operations in 1970. Two were in North Wales – the tiny Colwyn Bay Borough Council and Llandudno Urban District Council – and the rest in South Wales. Urban District Council bus operation was a feature of the Welsh bus scene; there were six bus operating UDCs in 1970.

Colwyn Bay ran just five single-deck buses in 1970, Bedfords, some with rare Spurling bodies. The borough obtained powers to run buses in 1926, and a promenade service was operated. Llandudno UDC started running buses in 1928, and famously favoured small Guys,

Top: Several Leyland Atlanteans were acquired with the James business, like this 1959 PDR1/1 with semi-lowheight Weymann 73-seat body, seen swinging out of the former James depot in Ammanford.
Geoff Lumb

Centre: As part of the Red & White group, United Welsh started with a mixed fleet but gradually the Bristol/ECW combination took over. This is a 1957 LS6G with 45-seat ECW body.
Geoff Lumb

Left: In 1964 the United Welsh coach fleet received two of these Bristol RELH6G with 47-seat ECW bodies.
Geoff Lumb

eight of which were in the 10-strong 1970 fleet along with two Dennises. The Guys included examples of the normal control Wolf, up to 20 years old, and the latest deliveries had been equally unusual Dennis Pax, bought in 1968.

The largest of the South Wales municipal fleets, perhaps inevitably, was City of Cardiff Transport, with 253 buses (230 double-deck, 23 single-deck), a varied mix of AEC, Daimler, Guy and Leyland chassis, with bodywork by Alexander, East Lancs, Longwell Green, MCW and Park Royal. In 1970 Cardiff's most recent deliveries had been Willowbrook-bodied Daimler Fleetlines and Alexander-bodied AEC Swifts.

Like so many municipal bus operators, Cardiff started with trams, in 1902, and in 1942 introduced its first trolleybuses; further trolleybus routes were introduced after World War 2 and the trams had been withdrawn by early in 1950. Cardiff experimented with a pay-on-entry system for its trams and most trolleybuses were delivered with front exits and rear entrances for a similar system. The motorbus fleet generally tended to be less standardised than many city fleets, and this situation would continue after 1970.

Next municipal operator in terms of size was Newport Corporation with 91 buses (83 double-deck, eight single-deck). Newport operated horse trams then electric trams, which disappeared by 1937. Motorbuses first appeared in 1924, and in 1970 Leylands dominated the fleet. In 1970 it received more Alexander-bodied Leyland Atlanteans, a type it had favoured since 1966.

Merthyr Tydfil was first served by company-owned trams but the corporation obtained powers to run motorbuses from 1924. The trams were abandoned in 1939. The 1970 fleet of 72 buses (41 double-deck, 31 single-deck) was 100 per cent Leyland, mostly with East Lancs bodywork, a popular choice in South Wales. Its last East Lancs-bodied Titan PD3s had been bought in 1966, and since that time it had bought East Lancs-bodied Leopards.

Pontypridd UDC had 40 buses in 1970 (26 double-deck, 14 single-deck), mostly AECs and Guys with bodies by a range of builders. Trams then motorbuses then trolleybuses were operated, but the trams were withdrawn in 1930 and the trolleybuses in 1957. Its newest buses in 1970 were late-model AEC Regent Vs with Willowbrook bodies, bought in 1969.

Aberdare UDC operated trams from 1913, was a short-lived trolleybus pioneer and operated motorbuses from the early 1920s. Like Pontypridd, it favoured Bristol chassis until these were no longer available outside the state-owned sector and turned to AECs and Guys. The 1970 fleet comprised 37 buses (5 double-deck, 31 single-deck, one minibus), and its newest deliveries were Willowbrook-bodied AEC Reliance single-deckers, new in 1968.

Left: Two very BET Group Leyland Tiger Cub PSUC1/1 at the Thomas Bros depot near Port Talbot, a 1953 example with Weymann 44-seat body on the left, and a 1961 Park Royal-bodied 45-seater on the right, complete with illuminated advertisement panel.
Geoff Lumb

Below: At Cwmtillery in 1973, a Jones, Aberbeeg Leyland Tiger Cub PSUC1/3 with Weymann body, new in 1960.
Mark Page

The West Monmouthshire Omnibus Board, known widely as West Mon, had a shorter history than the other local municipal fleets. In an area dominated by private operators, two local UDCs decided they wanted to operate buses, and in 1926 the West Mon Board was set up by Bedwelty and Mynyddislwyn urban councils. Initially West Mon ran routes acquired from other operators, but most famously had operated buses on the steep and awkward hill between Bargoed and Aberbargoed with specially-equipped buses. The 1970 fleet of 30 buses contained equal numbers of double-deckers and single-deckers, all on Leyland chassis. In 1970 it received further deliveries of Willowbrook-bodied Leyland Leopards, which had become its standard purchase.

Caerphilly UDC obtained powers to operate motorbuses in 1917, and by 1970 had 31 buses (15 double-deck, 16 single-deck), the majority Leylands with Massey bodies. Caerphilly latterly favoured Leopards, and it took delivery of a Northern Counties-bodied example during 1970.

Gelligaer UDC started motorbus services in 1928 and in 1970 its small fleet consisted of 27 buses (three double-deck, 23 single-deck, one minibus), mostly AECs. Its newest buses in 1970 were Willowbrook-bodied Swifts delivered two years earlier.

By far the smallest of the South Wales municipal operators was Bedwas & Machen UDC, which had operated motorbuses from 1917. It had just six buses in 1970 (five double-deck, one single-deck), mostly AECs with Massey bodies; its newest bus in 1970 was a 1968 Leyland Titan PD3 with Massey lowbridge bodywork.

Since 1970 – in some cases very soon after 1970 – the Welsh transport scene started to change, almost out of all recognition. The most recognisable elements today are Cardiff Bus and Newport Transport, two of the dwindling band of local authority-owned bus fleets in Britain. So what happened to the other Welsh municipals? One other has survived; Islwyn Borough Council is the renamed successor to the West Mon Board, but the others have disappeared into history. Merthyr Tydfil retained its name in the 1974 local government reorganisation, but competitive moves by the National Welsh company accelerated its demise in 1989. Three UDC operations, Bedwas & Machen, Caerphilly and Gelligaer, were merged into the new Rhymney Valley District Council in 1974, but this was bought by National Welsh in 1989. Pontypridd was renamed Taff-Ely District Council in 1974; it was bought by National Welsh in 1988. Aberdare UDC became Cynon Valley Borough Council in 1974, but suffered from local competition and sold out to Red & White in 1992.

The mentions of National Welsh also reflect changes that would affect the structure of the NBC-owned companies. With an

Above: A South Wales 1963 AEC Renown 3B3RA with Willowbrook 71-seat forward entrance body in Swansea. After the Renowns South Wales reverted to the Regent V, which it bought until 1967.
G Keepin

Left: On 1 January 1971 National Bus Company reorganised its company structure in South Wales, and the United Welsh, Thomas Bros and Neath & Cardiff businesses were placed under SWT control. This resulted in the unfamiliar sight of standard Tilling-issue Bristol/ECW types in South Wales colours. This 1965 RELL6G with 54-seat ECW body came from the United Welsh fleet.
Edward Shirras

inheritance of local companies serving South Wales it was probably inevitable that NBC would set about some form of rationalisation.

This started very quickly. In December 1970 Western Welsh took over its former BET Group stablemate, Rhondda, while in 1971/72 Western Welsh lost most of its operations in western Wales to the South Wales company. Western Welsh operations were now concentrated around Cardiff, Newport, Barry and the Valleys, often shared with Red & White. This essentially formed a group of companies, with Western Welsh/Rhondda, Red & White and Jones of Aberbeeg.

Further west, at the start of 1971 NBC tidied things up when South Wales Transport took control of the three neighbouring companies, Neath & Cardiff, Thomas Bros and United Welsh.

Later in the 1970s NBC created a new company, National Welsh, which took over Red & White and Western Welsh. This started in 1978 as a 700-strong giant, but by the time it was sold to its management under the NBC privatisation the fleet had dropped to 450. Although, as we have seen, National Welsh initially started out on the acquisition trail, buying up the Taff-Ely and Inter Valley Link (the renamed Rhymney Valley) operations, and virtually putting Merthyr Tydfil out of business, it was in financial trouble by the early 1990s. Its eastern part, trading as Red & White, was sold off to Western Travel, which created a new Red & White company. This wasn't enough, and National Welsh was effectively dismantled, with parts sold off to existing and new operators. It would be the most dramatic casualty of deregulation and privatisation.

In North Wales, Colwyn Bay became Colwyn Borough in 1974, but ceased operation in 1986, and Llandudno UDC became Aberconwy District Council in 1974.

As part of the preparation for privatisation it was decreed that NBC's larger companies would be split into smaller units, and that led to the break-up of the Crosville empire. The two companies that emerged produced English and Welsh Crosville companies; Crosville Wales Ltd, with 470 buses, was initially bought by its management team in 1987, and Crosville Motor Services Ltd, also with 470 buses, but with operations in Cheshire, the Wirral and South Merseyside, went to ATL in 1988. Subsequently both companies changed hands and have ended up as parts of the Arriva and First empires respectively. ∎

Above: Photographed after the 1971 transfer to South Wales Transport, a 1961 Bristol Lodekka FS6G with 60-seat ECW body.
Edward Shirras

Left: A Thomas Bros Leyland Tiger Cub PSUC1/1 with Weymann body, one of four bought in 1955, still in Thomas blue but with South Wales fleetnames in Port Talbot in April 1971.
Edward Shirras

Above: A Rhondda 1963 AEC Regent V 2MD3RA with 65-seat Northern Counties forward entrance bodywork at Pontypridd in 1972. Rhondda bought 18 similar buses in 1963/65.
Mark Page

Left: An older Rhondda Regent, a 1954 lightweight Regent III 6813S with Weymann 60-seat body, one of 10 delivered in that year.
Geoff Lumb

Below: At Newport bus station in April 1970, a 1963 Red & White Bristol Lodekka FS6G with ECW 60-seat body. The fleetnumber, L763, signifies that it was the seventh Lodekka delivered in 1963. This bus has a B-suffix registration mark; the first buses of this order had late-issue reversed registrations.
Mark Page

Newport bus station again and a Red & White Bristol RELL6G with 54-seat ECW bodywork featuring the early wraparound screen front. One of a batch of 11, the fleetnumber tells us that it is a 1965 delivery.
Geoff Lumb

One of the famous Neath & Cardiff 'brown bombers', the coaches used on the Swansea-Cardiff route, at Cardiff bus station. It is one of two AEC Reliance 4MU3RA with Duple Commander 49-seat bodies bought in 1965.
Geoff Lumb

Representing the tiny Colwyn Bay UDC fleet, the 1960 Bedford J2LZ2 with 21-seat Spurling body.
Geoff Lumb

Left: One of six Rhondda Leyland Atlantean PDR1/1 with Northern Counties 73-seat bodies that were bought in 1968, at Cardiff bus station.
M Street

Below: Ordered by Rhondda and delivered in Rhondda livery to Western Welsh in 1971, one of 10 Leyland Leopard PDU4A/4R with 45-seat Willowbrook bodywork.
Edward Shirras

Above: An earlier Red & White Bristol/ECW, a 1959 MW6G 45-seat bus.
G Mead

Below: In Gloucester bus station, a 1968 Red & White Bristol RELL6L with 53-seat ECW body of the shallow front screen style.
Edward Shirras

Above: The little Llandudno UDC fleet was well-known for its fleet of elderly small Guy buses, like this 1949 Wolf with 20-seat Barnard body seen alongside the track of the Great Orme cable tramway, also operated by the local council. This bus would remain in service well into the 1970s.
Geoff Lumb

Below: In the familiar surroundings of Cardiff bus station, a 1961 Cardiff Corporation AEC Regent V 2D3RV with 63-seat East Lancs body, one of 20 bought in 1961/62.
Mark Page

Cardiff's motorbus fleet was famously mixed, with examples of most current models. This Guy Arab V with 65-seat Alexander body was one of 22 bought in 1965/66 along with 15 30ft-long 70-seaters.
Geoff Lumb

Unusual Cardiff purchases in 1960 were six AEC/Park Royal Bridgemaster B3RA 68-seaters, and a freshly repainted example is seen in Cardiff bus station alongside another AEC, a Rhondda Regent V/Northern Counties.
Geoff Lumb

In Cardiff bus station in 1970, a 1969 Newport Corporation Leyland Atlantean PDR1A/1 with Alexander 74-seat body. After batches of Atlanteans Newport moved on to Scania buses, and has continued to favour that make.
Mark Page

Above: Late in 1970 Neath & Cardiff took delivery of two unusual AEC Reliance 6MU2R with bodies that were essentially to Plaxton's Derwent bus body design but with coach seats and extra external brightwork. These would prove to be the last new N&C coaches, as the company was absorbed into South Wales Transport on 1 January 1971.
G H Truran

Below: Like many municipal operators Cardiff tried dual-door rear-engined single-deckers in the late 1960s. This is a 1968 AEC Swift MP2R with 47-seat Alexander W type body featuring a front end design that was unique to Cardiff.
M J Kernick

Above: **Cardiff went for the Daimler Fleetline in a big way and this is a 1967 Metro-Cammell-bodied 75-seat example, one of 16 delivered in 1967/68.**
G Mead

Below: **In 1967 Newport bought eight of these Bristol RESL6L with 42-seat ECW bodies.**
M J Kernick

Above: Merthyr Tydfil bought 21 of these Leyland Titan PD3/4 with 73-seat East Lancs bodywork in 1958-61 and went on to buy forward entrance versions before moving to single-deckers. This 1960 example is seen at Merthyr.

Mark Page

Below: Pontypridd UDC favoured AEC and Guy buses. This is a 1967 AEC Regent V 2D3RA with Metro-Cammell 60-seat forward entrance body, in Pontypridd in 1972.

Mark Page

Left: Aberdare UDC also favoured AECs and Guys. This is a 1958 Guy Arab LUF with 44-seat Longwell Green body, one of four delivered in 1958.
Geoff Lumb

Below: The West Mon Board operated a number of Leyland Titans with lowbridge bodies by several builders. This is a 1958 PD2/40 with 55-seat Willowbrook body.
G Mead

Opposite above: **East Lancs-bodied Leyland Leopards became Merthyr Tydfil's choice and this is a 1971 PSU3A/2R 51-seater, in Cardiff.**
Michael Dryhurst

Left: **An AEC Reliance 2MU3RV in the Pontypridd fleet, one of two delivered in 1963 with 45-seat Longwell Green bodywork.**
T Walker

Above: **Another West Mon Leyland PD2/40, this time a 1965 Massey-bodied 55-seat lowbridge example.**
G H Truran

Left: Caerphilly UDC bought four of these Leyland Leopard PSU3/1 with 55-seat Massey bodies in 1962/64. This is a 1962 example, seen in Caerphilly.
Mark Page

Opposite below: At Ystrad Mynach in 1972, a Gelligaer UDC AEC Reliance 2MU3RA with Willowbrook 43-seat body, one of two bought in 1966.
Mark Page

Below: Bedwas & Machen UDC no.11 was a 1959 AEC Regent V MD3RV with Massey 58-seat lowbridge body, seen here in Bedwas.
Mark Page

Above: **Caerphilly UDC also bought this late-model Leyland Royal Tiger PSU1/13 with Massey 44-seat body. It was new in 1957, when other UK customers were buying Leyland's lighter Tiger Cub.**
Michael Dryhurst

Left: **A 1956 AEC Regent V MD3RV from the tiny Bedwas & Machen fleet, fitted with Longwell Green 55-seat lowbridge body.**
Michael Dryhurst

The South Midlands

Although the term is not as widely recognised as its eastern and western brothers, the South Midlands is defined by government as Northamptonshire, Bedfordshire and the northern part of Buckinghamshire. For the purposes of this book, we include those parts of the Home Counties beyond London Transport's reach plus Oxfordshire.

There were two major territorial NBC operators in this area in 1970, United Counties and City of Oxford, as well as just two municipal operators – and one of these would not survive the year.

United Counties, a former Tilling company, was based in Northampton and had an interesting history. Its roots were in the Wellingborough Motor Omnibus company, which in 1921 adopted the United Counties name. It became a Tilling Group company in 1931 and its geographical position meant that it lost and gained territory over the years. A major gain was the Midland Area of Tilling's Eastern National company which passed to United Counties in 1952, expanding its area to include areas like Aylesbury, Bedford and Luton and virtually doubling the fleet size.

In 1969 United Counties acquired the Bedfordshire and Northamptonshire services of Birch Bros, the long-established London area independent, and during 1970 it bought the Luton Corporation Transport undertaking.

As it was surrounded by other major territorial operations, United Counties services connected with those of the Tilling-owned Eastern Counties, Lincolnshire and Thames Valley companies, the BET-owned City of Oxford and Midland Red companies, and London Transport Country Area and Green Line routes.

In 1970 Northampton-based United Counties had 575 buses and coaches (367 double-deck, 146 single-deck, 62 coaches), mostly of Bristol/ECW manufacture, though the Birch acquisition had brought Leyland Leopards into the fleet, and there would be Bristol REs, Dennis Lolines, Leyland Lowlanders and Titans from the Luton fleet. The newest pure United Counties buses in the 1970 fleet were Bristols, RE coaches and buses, LH buses and VRT double-deckers.

City of Oxford Motor Services Ltd grew out of a horse tramway system that was taken over by a BET subsidiary with a view to running electric trams. This never happened and motorbuses soon became the main form of public transport in the city and throughout Oxfordshire and into the surrounding areas. Like United Counties, City of Oxford services connected with a range of other operators – Aldershot & District, Bristol Omnibus, London Transport, Midland Red, Thames Valley, United Counties and Wilts & Dorset.

For years the City of Oxford company was synonymous with the products of AEC and its 218-strong fleet in 1970 (126 double-deck, 90 single-deck, two coaches) included 188 AECs as well as five Dennis Lolines and 25 Daimlers. The last new AECs for the fleet would be Reliances bought in 1971, and the last double-deck AECs were Renowns bought in 1967, which followed a long line of Regents. From 1968 City of Oxford turned to Daimler Fleetlines for its double-deck requirements, and between 1968 and 1972 received 59 with Alexander or Northern Counties double-deck bodies, many to two-door layout, and one single-deck version was delivered in 1970.

Following the 1970 acquisition of Luton's Corporation bus operation by United Counties there was just one municipal operator left in the South Midlands, Northampton Corporation. This small operation, just 68 double-deckers in 1970, acquired the local horse tram operation, electrified it, and had replaced it with motorbuses by 1934. The 1970 fleet was highly standardised on 68 Roe-bodied Daimler CVG6s, the last bought in 1968, and Northampton was notable for clinging on to 27ft-long rear-entrance double-deckers long after most fleets. Its next new buses, in 1973, would be Willowbrook-bodied Daimler Fleetline single-deckers, and these would be followed by Leyland Nationals.

In the National Bus Company privatisation, United Counties was one of the first sales to Stagecoach, and City of Oxford initially went to its management team, but is now a member of the Go-Ahead Group. Northampton Corporation was bought by GRT Holdings, and following GRT's merger with Badgerline the local services are run by FirstGroup. ■

Looking slightly uncomfortable in Tilling green United Counties livery in the company of Bristol Lodekkas, an ex-Luton Corporation 1960 Leyland Titan PD2/30 with East Lancs 55-seat lowbridge body, at Vauxhall Motors in Luton in June 1970.
J Wood

The big 1970 news at United Counties was the acquisition of the Luton Corporation undertaking, which brought a mix of standard and non-standard types into the UCOC fleet. This 1970 Bristol RELL6L with 48-seat dual-door body was delivered to Luton Corporation just before the take-over. It was one of 30 similar REs acquired at the time, and another 10 that had been on order went directly to UCOC.
Geoff Lumb

More unusual acquisitions from Luton Corporation included Leyland Titans and Lowlanders. This is a 1962 LR7 Lowlander with 65-seat East Lancs forward entrance body, in full UCOC livery.
Geoff Lumb

Representing the old order at United Counties that was on its way out in 1970, a 1952 Bristol LWL5G with 39-seat ECW body, acquired with Eastern National's Midland operation.
Geoff Lumb

City of Oxford bought eight of these AEC Reliance 2MU3RV with 44-seat Marshall bodies in 1962/63. Note the distinctive vee decoration on the front panelling in this 1972 Oxford view.
Ted Jones

A former Aldershot & District 1961 AEC Reliance 2MU3RV with dual-purpose 41-seat Park Royal bodywork, looking smart in the distinctive colours of its new owner, City of Oxford, in 1970.
Ted Jones

After many years buying Regents, City of Oxford moved on to the lowheight AEC Bridgemaster and Renown in the 1960s, like this 1966 3B3RA model with forward-entrance Park Royal 65-seat body, seen in 1972.
Ted Jones

This bus was one of five Bristol LHS6P with 37-seat ECW bodies that had an interesting early history. New to Luton Corporation in 1969, but not used, they were acquired by United Counties with that undertaking, but still not used, and were transferred to fellow NBC company, Eastern Counties. This is no.134 in Luton livery with registration XXE 134H, but this mark was surrendered and it was re-registered by Eastern Counties as WNG 104H.

G R Mills

After many years buying the mid-engined AEC Reliance, City of Oxford moved on to AEC's rear-engined Swift, like this 1966 MP2R model with Willowbrook 53-seat body, seen at Christ Church, Oxford.

N J R Taylor

Above: **City of Oxford** connected with the former London Transport Country Area at Aylesbury, where this 1960 AEC Regent V MD3RV with Willowbrook 63-seat body is seen.
Michael Dryhurst

Left: In transition – a 1957 Leyland Titan PD2/31 with 55-seat Weymann body still in Luton Corporation livery with its Luton fleetnumber, 151, on the front, near the United Counties 811 plate.
J Wood

Above: A memory of the Luton Corporation fleet before the United Counties take-over – a 1959 Leyland Titan PD2/22 with lowbridge Weymann 55-seat body seen in 1967.
Tony Wilson

Right: Northampton Corporation had a highly-standardised fleet for many years – Roe-bodied Daimler CVG6 double-deckers – and this was numerically the last of these to be delivered, one of five in 1968, that were also the last front-engined Daimlers for the UK market.
Malcolm Flynn

Below: Northampton later adopted a livery with more cream, as seen on a 1959 CVG6/Roe in 1975.
Mark Page

Left: Representing the earlier Northampton Daimler CVG6/Roe deliveries, this is a 1953 example.
Geoff Lumb

Below: Although North Wales and South Wales was dominated by large territorial operators, there was apparently still room for a surprising number of independents, often well-established firms with services connecting villages with market towns. Clynnog & Trevor Motor Co takes its name from two villages in Caernarvonshire and still survives – although Trevor has become Trefor in the Welsh spelling. This former Maidstone & District 1958 AEC Reliance MU3RV with 42-seat Harrington body, is seen in Caernarvon Square in 1973.
Malcolm Flynn

Further south, in Carmarthenshire, the 13-strong West Wales of Ammanford fleet included this Plaxton Derwent-bodied Leyland Leopard PSU3/3R, bought new in 1967 and seen in Ammanford.
Mark Page

Another view of one of the final batch
of Northampton Corporation Daimler
CVG6/Roe, seen when new in 1968.
T W Moore

The East Midlands

Our 'East Midlands' covers the area traditionally regarded as the East Midlands – Derbyshire, Leicestershire, and Nottinghamshire (not forgetting Rutland) – but also includes Lincolnshire. From the transport point of view there is no single dominant operator, but rather a good selection of medium-sized operators, many in the 300-400-vehicle range, including municipalities, NBC operators from both the BET and Tilling camps, and one significant independent.

Starting in the east, the Lincolnshire Road Car company covered a substantial area, centred on Lincoln, and with garages from Goole in the north to Grantham in the south.

Formed in 1928 around the Silver Queen company, the LMS and LNE railways acquired shareholdings in Lincolnshire in 1929 and the company grew through acquisition and the allocation of the local services of the once-massive United Automobile Services company. As a Tilling Group company from 1942 Lincolnshire received increasing quantities of Bristol/ECW products, and its 1970 fleet of 378 (132 double-deck, 231 single-deck, 15 coaches) consisted entirely of this combination, save for a handful of Bedford/Duple coaches.

The Bristol/ECW products included LHs, Lodekkas, MWs, RELHs, RELLs, and VRTs. Deliveries in 1970 were LH buses, two-door RELL buses, VRT double-deckers and Bedford VAM70/Duple coaches.

There were two municipal operators in Lincolnshire, Grimsby & Cleethorpes Transport Joint Committee and Lincoln City Transport. As the name suggests, Grimsby and Cleethorpes had separate municipal transport undertakings until they were amalgamated in 1957. Grimsby Corporation had acquired the local tramway operation in 1925 and replaced the trams with trolleybuses and motorbuses. A joint trolleybus route was started with nearby Cleethorpes Corporation. Cleethorpes had started running motorbuses in 1930 and bought its local tramway system in 1936. It replaced the trams with trolleybuses in 1937.

Grimsby-Cleethorpes Transport assumed control of the two undertakings in 1957, and in 1970 its fleet totalled 108 buses (65 double-deck, 43 single-deck). AECs and Daimlers were favoured, including AEC Reliances, Swifts, Regents and Bridgemasters, and Daimler CVG6-30s and Fleetlines, including single-deck examples. The most recent deliveries in 1970 were Roe-bodied Swifts and Fleetlines.

Lincoln City Transport acquired the local horse tram operation and introduced electric trams from 1905. Motorbuses appeared from 1920 and Leylands were favoured for many years. In the 1970 fleet of 58 buses (26 double-deck, 32 single-deck) were Tiger Cubs, Panthers, Titans and Atlanteans, with Roe bodies, the most recent deliveries being Panthers delivered in 1967-70.

East of Lincolnshire, Derbyshire and Nottinghamshire were home to several interesting bus operations. The largest operator in the area by fleet size was Nottingham City Transport, with the independent Barton Transport and the NBC's Midland General and Trent close behind.

In 1970 Nottingham City Transport had 412 buses (402 double-deck, 10 single-deck), and like so many operators had started out with trams, moving on to motorbuses in the 1920s. Nottingham also moved on to trolleybuses, which it operated between 1927 and 1966. Its bus fleet was for many years well-known for its slightly quirky own-design buses, and in the 1960s Nottingham had bought AEC Renowns, Daimler Fleetlines and Leyland Atlanteans with a range of bodies. Its newest buses in 1970 were Northern Counties-bodied two-door Atlanteans.

In 1968 Nottingham City Transport had bought the neighbouring West Bridgford UDC undertaking, which brought AEC Swifts and more Renowns into the fleet.

Barton Transport was a pioneering bus operator, starting services in the 1900s and building up a substantial business. By 1970 Barton had 330 buses and although it had been notable for the wide range of secondhand buses and coaches acquired, as well as the many unusual new and converted buses it had owned. By 1970 the fleet was becoming standardised with substantial injections of AEC, Bedford and Leyland single-deckers with coach bodies.

Barton, based in Chilwell, had bus routes that radiated out to Derbyshire and Leicestershire, with frequent services Nottingham with Castle Donington, Derby, Leicester and Loughborough, as well as a long-distance services and extended tours.

The BET Group's main operation in the area was Trent Motor Traction, which in 1970 had 363

With many deep rural routes, Lincolnshire bought small buses like this 1970 Bristol LHS6P with 34-seat ECW body, seen in Lincoln bus station.
M Bennett

buses (172 double-deck, 146 single-deck, 45 coaches). Trent's roots date back to 1913, and for many years it bought BMMO-built buses from fellow BET company, Midland Red. Its 1970 fleet included many Leylands – Tiger Cubs, Leopards, Titans, Atlanteans – as well as Bristol REs and Daimler Fleetlines. Its most recent deliveries in 1970 were Leopard buses and coaches and Fleetline/Alexander double-deckers.

Trent, based in Derby, operated a network of frequent services linking centres like Derby with Alfreton and Nottingham, and Nottingham with Chesterfield and Mansfield.

The Tilling fleets in the area shared an unusual background. Mansfield District Traction had started as a tram operator in 1905 but the trams had been replaced by motorbuses by 1932 and five years later the company was bought by Balfour Beatty's Midland Counties Electric Supply company. This company already owned the Midland General Omnibus Co and the Nottingham & Derbyshire Traction company.

The Notts & Derby company started operating trams in 1913 between Nottingham and Ripley and in 1916 took over Ilkeston Corporation's Cotmanhay-Hallam Fields tram route. The trams were replaced by trolleybuses in 1933 and the two former tram routes were linked. Another 20 years later and the trolleybuses were replaced by motorbuses.

In 1920 Notts & Derby had set up the Midland General

Left: Grimsby Cleethorpes bought Daimler Fleetlines from 1965 and from 1969 these had Roe 74-seat dual-door bodies, like this example, one of eight bought in 1970.
Geoff Lumb

Below: Variety in the Lincoln Corporation fleet, with a line-up headed by a 1951 Roe-bodied Leyland Titan PD2/10, followed by one of the 1948 Guy Arab III/Guys and a Roe-bodied Leyland Atlantean.
Geoff Lumb

Also based in Derbyshire, but right at the northern end of the East Midlands with services within the area and north into Yorkshire, was East Midland Motor Services, based at Chesterfield. This had its roots in one of the bus businesses set up by W T Underwood, bought in 1929 by the LMS and LNER railway companies; in 1930 BET bought a controlling interest.

East Midland's route network stretched into Nottinghamshire, with regular services from Chesterfield to Nottingham and Mansfield, and into Yorkshire with services to Doncaster and Rotherham from Chesterfield and Worksop, and between Chesterfield and Sheffield.

The 1970 East Midland fleet of 230 buses (80 double-deck, 120 single-deck, 18 dual-purpose, 12 coaches) was composed largely of Leylands of different types, but with some AECs, Bristols and Bedfords as well. The most recent purchases had been Alexander-bodied Leyland Atlanteans and AEC Swift, and Bristol LH and RE single-deckers.

Omnibus company to operate motorbuses and although the Notts & Derby name survived the trolleybuses, Midland General became the principal operator.

With the nationalisation of the electricity industry the British Electricity Authority concluded a deal with the new British Transport Commission in 1948 and Mansfield District, Midland General and Notts & Derby found themselves under Tilling control.

As Tilling companies their fleets gradually included more Bristol/ECW products; in 1970 they had FS, FSF and LD Lodekkas, as well as LHs, MWs and REs. The latest deliveries, in 1969/70, were LH and RELL single-deckers and VRT double-deckers. By 1970 the three companies were under Midland General control with a combined fleet size of 321 (212 double-deck, 87 single-deck, 22 coaches).

Based at Heanor, the Midland General companies operated frequent services in an area bounded by Nottingham, Mansfield, Chesterfield, Matlock and Ripley.

There were two municipal operators in Derbyshire in 1970. The bigger one was Derby Corporation, which had a fleet of 144 double-deck buses, all but three of which were Daimlers; most of the bodies were built by Roe. Derby Corporation took over the local company-owned horse trams in 1899, introduced electric trams from 1904 and motorbuses in the 1920s. In the 1930s Derby turned to trolleybuses for its main routes, but these were finally withdrawn in 1967.

Derby's 1970 fleet largely comprised Daimler CVG6s and Fleetlines, and in 1970 it received further deliveries of Roe-bodied Fleetlines.

Chesterfield Corporation bought the local horse tramway company in 1897 and electrified it in 1904, but abandoned the trams in favour of trolleybuses in 1927 and these had been withdrawn by 1938.

The 1970 Chesterfield fleet of 139 vehicles was made up of 74 double-deck and 65 single-deck buses, a mix of AECs, Daimlers and Leylands. Although it had been an early customer for

Left: A former Southern Vectis 1953 Bristol LS6G with ECW coach body, in use with Lincolnshire as a bus in Grantham in 1969.
Edward Shirras

Centre: Grimsby Cleethorpes also bought dual-door Daimler Fleetline single-deckers in 1966/67, SRG6LWs with Willowbrook 42-seat bodies. This is a 1967 example at Cleveland Bridge when new.
M Fowler

Below: On a wet day outside Lincoln railway station, a newly-delivered Leyland Panther PSUR1/1 with 49-seat Roe body in 1968.
Gavin Booth

Leyland's Atlantean, in the 1960s it embarked on a move to driver-only operation using dual-door single-deckers. In 1967-69 it bought Daimler Roadliners and Leyland Panthers but would revert to double-deckers in the 1970s.

South to Leicestershire and another significant municipality, Leicester City Transport. The corporation bought the local horse tramway company in 1901, converted to electric cars in 1904/05 and abandoned them between 1939 and 1949, switching to motorbuses, which had first appeared in the fleet in 1925.

With 202 buses in the 1970 fleet (169 double-deck, 33 single-deck), the Leicester fleet had become known for its variety. In the 1960s it had bought Leyland Titan PD3s with East Lancs, Metro-Cammell and Park Royal bodies, AEC Renowns with East Lancs bodies, Leyland Atlanteans with ECW, Metro-Cammell and Park Royal bodies and Bristol RELLs with ECW bodies. The newest deliveries, in 1969/70, were Atlanteans and RELLs.

The main territorial company operator in Leicestershire was the mighty Midland Red, which is covered under the West Midlands.

Changes in the East Midlands area started soon after 1970. Control of the Midland General company passed to Trent in 1972 and had been fully absorbed by 1976. Also in 1972 Trent had grown with the takeover of the Buxton and Matlock depots of NBC's North Western Road Car company when Selnec PTE acquired much of the North Western operation. Trent passed to its management team in 1986 during the NBC sell-off and survived acquisition by any of the major groups to grow into a highly-respected quality operation; following the acquisition of the Barton Transport bus business, it trades as Trent Barton. Mansfield District was passed into East Midland

Left: Nottingham's single-deckers also carried unusually-styled bodies. This substantial-looking bus is a 1969 AEC Swift 2MP2R with dual-door Northern Counties 43-seat body. The six buses in this batch were sold on to Grimsby Cleethorpes in 1975.
M Tubb

Below: Before it embarked on an all-single-deck policy, Barton Transport acquired interesting secondhand double-deckers including this 1963 AEC Renown 3B2RA with Park Royal 74-seat body. It was new to Smith, Barrhead, and is seen at Ilkeston bus station.
T Hartley

control in 1972 as part of the NBC rationalisation scheme of the time. East Midland is now part of Stagecoach.

Lincolnshire Road Car was sold to Yorkshire Traction in 1988 and survived successfully until 2005 when it passed with the Traction Group to Stagecoach. It had bought the independent, Gash of Newark in 1989.

One of the municipal operators survives in the dwindling list of local authority-owned companies; Nottingham City Transport is England's largest local authority fleet, with a minority shareholding by the international transport group Transdev, and an involvement in the new Nottingham trams; in 1991 Nottingham had bought the independent South Notts business. The others have been absorbed into the large groups, Derby, which in 1973 had bought the independent, Blue Bus of Willington, into what is now Arriva, Leicester into First, and Chesterfield and Grimsby-Cleethorpes into Stagecoach. ∎

Sitting at Lincoln Corporation's St Marks garage, one of 25 Roe-bodied Leyland Panthers bought in 1967-70. This is a 1970 PSUR1A/1.
Geoff Lumb

Nottingham City Transport had very individual views on bus design and layout, and this is typified by a 1965 Leyland Atlantean PDR1/2 with Nottingham-styled Metro-Cammell 72-seat body, one of 22 bought in 1965.
Mark Page

Heading a line-up in Nottingham's Lower Parliament Street depot is a 1954 AEC Regent III 9613S with Park Royal 53-seat lowbridge body.
Geoff Lumb

Above: Instantly recognisable as a Barton Transport bus, a 1947 Leyland Titan PD1 with Duple lowbridge forward entrance 55-seat body, at Huntingdon Street, Nottingham in 1969.
Mark Page

Left: Like Nottingham City, Barton Transport had unusual views on bus design, that produced this unique vehicle, the 1960 Dennis Loline III with lowbridge Northern Counties 68-seat body; combining a lowheight chassis and a lowbridge body produced an extra-low (12.5ft high) bus.
Geoff Lumb

Above: Barton also acquired former London Transport buses like the former RTL810, a Leyland Titan PD2, seen outside the company's Ilkeston garage in 1969. Note the 'Barton' radiator badge, replacing the original 'London Transport' one.
Edward Shirras

Left: An earlier Trent Leopard/Willowbrook, a 1965 PSU3/1R with 51-seat dual-purpose body, at Derby bus station.
P Yeomans

Right: A 1967 Trent Daimler Fleetline/Alexander 77-seater at Derby alongside a 1961 Leyland Tiger Cub PSUC1/1 with 41-seat Willowbrook body.
T W W Knowles

At Ilkeston in 1969, a newly-delivered Midland General Bristol VRTSL6G with 70-seat ECW body.
Edward Shirras

Variety at Chesterfield Corporation's Stonegravels depot, with, from the left, a 1964 Daimler CCG6 with Weymann 65-seat forward-entrance body, a 1961 Leyland Titan PD2A/30 with 58-seat Weymann lowbridge body, and two Leyland Titan PD2/30s, dating from 1958 and 1960, with Weymann bodies.
Roger Kaye

The deep windows of the East Lancs 74-seat body on this AEC Renown 3B3RA suit the Leicester livery. It was one of seven delivered in 1965/66 and is seen in 1968.
G Mead

Above: **After buying Leyland Titan and Atlantean double-deckers, Trent switched to Daimler Fleetlines in 1963, and this is a 1969 CRG6LX with Alexander 77-seat body, at Huntingdon Street, Nottingham when new.**
Mark Page

Below: **An earlier Trent Daimler Fleetline, new in 1963 with Northern Counties 77-seat body, at Derby bus station in 1967. Note the position of the registration plate.**
Tony Wilson

Trent also received standard BET-style single-deckers, including this 1969 Leyland Leopard PSU3A/4R with Willowbrook 49-seat body.
Geoff Lumb

Mansfield District buses were easily distinguished from other Tilling Group buses by the unusual application of the green/cream livery. Here are two Bristol/ECW products, a 1960 Lodekka FD6G with 60-seat body, and a 1955 LS6G 43-seater.
Geoff Lumb

Mansfield District also received Bristol FLF6G Lodekkas with 70-seat ECW bodies.
Geoff Lumb

Left: Midland General's buses were also unusual in the Tilling family with their impressive blue/cream livery. This is a 1967 Bristol Lodekka FLF6G with 70-seat ECW body in Nottingham in 1969.
Mark Page

Right: Some idea of the variety that could be seen in Nottingham is provided by this photo of a Midland General 1953 Bristol KSW6G with 60-seat ECW body, alongside a South Notts Northern Counties-bodied Leyland Titan PD3/4.
Geoff Lumb

Below: A very Tilling-looking back end on a bus owned by the former BET fleet, East Midland. At Nottingham in 1969 is a Bristol RELL6G/ECW 49-seater, one of 12 delivered in 1967/68.
Mark Page

Derby Corporation was another fleet that favoured Roe-bodied Daimlers. This is a 1964 CVG6 with 65-seat body; Derby bought 47 similar buses between 1961 and 1965.
Mark Page

A mix of East Midland buses including a Leyland Tiger Cub/Weymann, a Bristol RELL6G/ECW and, on the right, a 1966 Leyland-Albion Lowlander LR7 with 70-seat Metro-Cammell forward entrance body.
Geoff Lumb

At first glance a BET standard-issue AEC Reliance or Leyland Leopard, this is a rear-engined AEC Swift MP2R with 45-seat Marshall body, one of eight supplied to East Midland in 1967/68.
Geoff Lumb

From Daimler CVG6s, Derby progressed to Daimler Fleetlines, again with Roe bodies. This is a 1969 delivery, a 78-seater.
Geoff Lumb

A Chesterfield Corporation 1962
Daimler Fleetline CRG6LX with
77-seat Metro-Cammell body in
the beautiful North Derbyshire
countryside near Hundall.
Roger Kaye

Representing the old and new
faces of Leicester City Transport
in Charles Street, Leicester in
July 1970 – a 1961 Leyland Titan
PD3A/1 with Metro-Cammell
74-seat body and a 1969 Bristol
RELL6L with 47-seat dual-door
ECW body, one of 20 delivered
in 1969/70.
Mark Page

Another Leicester Leyland Titan
PD3A/1, this time with Park Royal
74-seat body and dating from 1966.
Geoff Lumb

Outside Leicester's Abbey Park Road depot, a Leyland Atlantean PDR1A/1 with 74-seat ECW body, one of 10 delivered in 1968. The Leicester livery only serves to emphasise the ungainly proportions of the normal-height ECW body of the time.
Geoff Lumb

The independent fleet of Gash, Newark, was well-known for its Daimler double-deckers, and these three CVD6s are, from the left, a 1950 Duple-bodied lowbridge 57-seater, a 1948 Roberts-bodied 56-seater and a 1949 Duple-bodied lowbridge 53-seater.
Geoff Lumb

Wearing the distinctive livery of the Gotham-based independent, South Notts, at Broad Marsh, Nottingham in 1969, a 1958 Leyland Titan PD3/4 with lowbridge Weymann 67-seat body.
Mark Page

The West Midlands

The Government Offices for the English Regions define the West Midlands as an area stretching from Stoke-on-Trent in the north to Hereford and Evesham in the south, from Shrewsbury in the west to Rugby and Burton-on-Trent in the east. In other words, a substantial part of England, particularly when you realise that its present-day population of 5.2 million is roughly 9 per cent of the UK total, and broadly the same as Scotland's.

It is of course an area readily associated with heavy engineering, certainly in 1970, but three-quarters of the region's area is made up of rural counties, housing two-fifths of the population.

Birmingham inevitably dominates the West Midlands, and for many years, including 1970, it was home to two of the largest bus companies in the UK. One, the newly-created West Midlands PTE, had already swallowed up the municipal bus operations in Birmingham, Walsall, West Bromwich and Wolverhampton, and could boast a combined fleet of 2,078 buses (including 48 trolleybuses inherited from Walsall). The other, Midland Red – the Birmingham & Midland Motor Omnibus Co Ltd, to give it its Sunday name – had a fleet of 1,761 buses in 1970, but would shrink to barely 1,000 buses by the end of the decade, and would be dismembered shortly after that.

The creation of West Midlands PTE in 1969 heralded major changes in the ownership of local buses. Birmingham City

Birmingham City Transport buses inevitably dominated the initial fleet of the new West Midlands PTE in 1969, and included many of the standard buses delivered in the early 1950s. On the famous 11 Outer Circle route at Perry Barr is a Daimler CVG6 with 55-seat Crossley body, one of a large batch delivered in 1953/54. The WM logo has replaced the BCT crest.
Malcolm Flynn

Transport had been the principal transport operator in the rapidly expanding city since the early years of the 20th century, particularly after 1911 when it acquired the important City of Birmingham Tramways company. Motorbus services started in 1913 and in 1922 Birmingham introduced trolleybuses on the Nechells route.

Trams were abandoned between 1930 and 1953, and the trolleybuses had gone by 1951, leaving the vast fleet of highly-standardised motorbuses to serve the city. Locally-built Daimlers, often with locally-built Metro-Cammell bodies, were favoured from the 1930s, with smaller batches of AECs, Crossleys, Guys and Leylands to make up the numbers. The bus fleet peaked in the 1950s with over 1,800 buses, but at the time the PTE was formed, Birmingham's contribution was under 1,500 buses.

Like London and other major cities, Birmingham had developed its own distinct motorbus design, and had taken massive deliveries of these between 1947 and 1954 – so many that it would not require new buses until the early 1960s. After a few experimental Leyland Atlanteans these were Daimler Fleetlines with Metro-Cammell or Park Royal bodies, and Fleetlines would be Birmingham's – and the PTE's – standard fare well into the 1970s. Single-deckers never played an important part in Birmingham, but in the 1960s BCT had bought Marshall-bodied Fleetline single-deckers, Metro-Cammell-bodied two-door AEC Swifts and unusual Strachan-bodied Ford R192s.

Walsall Corporation started direct tramway operations in 1904, but the trams had been replaced by 1933, first by motorbuses and from 1931 by trolleybuses. Unlike Birmingham, Walsall stuck with its trolleybuses – but the 48 inherited by the new PTE in 1969 would last only until 1970.

The Walsall undertaking became well-known for its varied and unusual fleet, a consequence of the many experiments and innovations introduced during the long reign of R Edgley Cox as general manager; he joined the undertaking in 1952 and briefly moved to the new PTE as chief engineer. Cox is remembered for his 30ft-long trolleybuses (the first buses to this length on two axles, in 1954), extra-short Fleetlines and heavy rebuilds of existing buses. The last deliveries, in 1969, were the last of the short Northern Counties Fleetlines.

West Bromwich was the smallest of the corporation fleets absorbed into the PTE in 1969, with some 130 buses. It never operated its own trams, but leased the system to company operators until 1924 when Birmingham City Transport took these over, operating trams into West Bromwich for a further 15 years.

Motorbus operation started in 1914 and, like Birmingham, Daimlers dominated the fleet, many with Metro-Cammell bodies. The newest deliveries had been ECW-bodied Fleetlines in 1969.

Wolverhampton Corporation acquired and electrified its local tramways, operated buses continuously from 1911, and ran a substantial trolleybus fleet between 1923 and 1967. Like Birmingham it favoured locally-built buses, in its case Guy Arab motorbuses and Sunbeam trolleybuses. Its most recent purchases, prior to the formation of the PTE, were Guy Arab Vs in 1965 and a Ford R226 with two-door Strachans body in 1966.

Outwardly anonymous, the only clue that this is a West Midland PTE bus is the discreet letter 'H' that has been added under the fleetnumber. This is a former West Bromwich Corporation Daimler Fleetline CRG6LX with 73-seat ECW body, one of seven delivered in 1969; this bus was numerically West Bromwich's last new bus.
Tony Moyes

The WM logo has been applied to the former livery of this Guy Arab V with Park Royal 72-seat forward entrance body, one of 25 delivered to Wolverhampton Corporation in 1963. It is seen in 1971 at Penn, Wolverhampton.
Mark Page

Among the UK's municipal bus fleets, Birmingham City Transport had been the largest, with nearly 1,500 buses in 1969 to Manchester's 1,250, but with 2,078 buses, West Midlands PTE had a smaller fleet than the 2,700 of Selnec, serving the Greater Manchester conurbation, as Selnec encompassed a greater range of municipal fleets.

But the West Midlands also housed the National Bus Company's largest fleet, Midland Red with 1,761 buses, some 500 buses more than its nearest rival, the new London Country company. The 1970 fleet comprised 836 double-deckers, 773 single-deckers and 152 coaches.

Midland Red was one of the great and most highly individual of Britain's territorial bus companies. Its roots go back to a horsebus operator, the Birmingham & District Omnibus Company, which experimented with motorbuses briefly in 1904, but abandoned them. In 1912 the Birmingham & Midland Motor Omnibus company was registered and started running motorbuses in Birmingham. These again were short-lived and in 1914 Birmingham Corporation acquired the buses and took over the local route network that had been operated. This led to BMMO starting country routes and laying the basis for what became a massive operating area; this stretched from Shrewsbury and Hereford in the west, to Stafford and Burton-on-Trent in the north, to Leicester, Northampton and Rugby in the east, and to Banbury and Worcester in the south. Even then, longer-distance routes stretched its territory to centres like Gloucester and Nottingham, and its express services went further still, to London and to resorts in East Anglia and Wales.

There were high-frequency services throughout the Midland Red area, though the greatest concentration of buses was in the Black Country, west of Birmingham, to places like Dudley, Halesowen and Kidderminster.

Midland Red famously built its own buses, from 1924 right through until 1968. It had started with Tilling-Stevens petrol-electric types, but from 1924 developed its own range of single-deck types to serve its growing network of urban, rural and interurban routes, as well as for coaching duties. From the early 1930s it also built its own double-deckers. Although its early buses often appeared quirky when compared with buses from the major builders, during and after World War 2 Midland Red pioneered many concepts that would come to be widely accepted, including independent front suspension, disc brakes, and single-deckers with underfloor-mounted engines – and it designed and built its own engines too.

Although proprietary types were also bought from time to time, usually to meet vehicle shortages, for years the bulk of the Midland Red fleet was home-built. The first indications of a change of direction had come in 1962/63 when 100 Leyland Leopard single-deckers and 50 Daimler Fleetline double-deckers were bought. Midland Red continued to build its D9 double-decker until 1966, and its very last bus, an S23 single-decker, was actually completed in 1970. So while the 1970 fleet still included a substantial fleet of BMMO-built buses, the Leopard and Fleetline were quickly becoming the standard purchases until the advent of the Leyland National in 1972.

Midland Red also had its associated fleet, Stratford-upon-Avon Blue Motors, known as Stratford Blue. This company had started services out of Stratford in the 1920s, but passed into Balfour Beatty control in 1931; four years later the business passed to BMMO. Interestingly, it wasn't stocked with BMMO products, but in recent years had bought Leylands; the 1970 fleet was all-Leyland, 43 vehicles (18 double-deck, 19 single-deck, six coaches).

Stratford Blue services radiated out from Stratford to Birmingham, Banbury, Leamington Spa, Evesham, Cheltenham and Oxford. Its newest buses in 1970 were Leyland Atlanteans bought in 1967, and a Leyland Leopard bought in 1970. Five Leyland Panthers were delivered late in 1970, but by this time it had been decided that Stratford Blue would be absorbed into the parent Midland Red fleet, and they were never operated; instead Midland Red sold them to Preston Corporation in 1971.

Outside the West Midlands conurbation, there were other

Left: The discreet 'L' after the fleetnumber indicates that this is a former Walsall Corporation bus in the WMPTE fleet. It is a 1960 Dennis Loline II with Willowbrook 74-seat forward entrance body, and is seen at Cannock early in 1970.
Tony Moyes

Above: WMPTE also inherited the remnants of Walsall Corporation's trolleybus system, and here early in 1970 is a 1950 BUT 9611T with Northern Coachbuilders body. It had been new to Grimsby Cleethorpes, but was acquired by Walsall in 1961 who lengthened it to 30ft and rebuilt it as a 69-seat forward-entrance bus a couple of years later.
J Hardwick, via Malcolm Flynn

Right: Two former Walsall Corporation buses in WMPTE days, a rather grubby 1960 Dennis Loline II/Willowbrook in Walsall blue and a 1963 Daimler CVG6/Metro-Cammell in PTE livery.
Geoff Lumb

municipal bus fleets. The nearest was Coventry, where in 1912 the corporation had bought the local tramway company, which had introduced electric trams as early as 1895. Coventry Corporation started running motorbuses in 1914 and gradually built up the fleet, mainly locally-built Daimlers. The tramway system had to be abandoned following the devastating air raid on the city in November 1940 but the undertaking continued to operate and bought a substantial fleet of Daimler CV types, most with locally-built Metro-Cammell bodies, until 1963 when it surprised many observers by buying Leyland Atlanteans. There would be only one batch of these, in 1964, and Coventry switched to Daimler Fleetlines. The newest deliveries, between 1966 and 1970, had bodies by various builders – East Lancs, Neepsend, ECW and Park Royal. Coventry also bought ECW-bodied Bristol RESL single-deckers. The 1970 fleet consisted of 332 buses (299 double-deck, 30 single-deck, 3 coaches).

North of Coventry lies Burton-on-Trent, which in 1970 had its own corporation bus undertaking. This had started in 1905 as an electric tramway operator, but turned to buses in the 1920s and withdrew its trams in 1929. Unlike Coventry, which favoured Daimlers, Burton favoured Guys, built just 28 miles away in Wolverhampton. The last front-engined double-deckers for the fleet were Daimler CCG5s, essentially Daimlers with Guy gearboxes, bought in 1968, and then it turned to Daimler Fleetline single-deckers in 1969 and double-deckers in 1970. Its fleet in 1970 consisted of 45 buses (43 double-deck, two single-deck).

North-west of Burton lies the heavily-populated Potteries area, mainly served by the former BET operator, Potteries Motor Traction, known by its fleetname PMT. Its roots were in the BET's Potteries Electric Traction company, which had acquired a former steam tram operation in 1896, converting it to electric traction from 1899. Motorbuses were tried in the early years, but with more success from 1913/14; these were useful to compete with the many independent bus operators in the area, and buses had replaced the trams by 1928.

PMT acquired most of its smaller competitors, which brought even more variety into a fleet that was never noted for its

standardisation. Recent deliveries in 1970 included AEC Reliance and Leyland Leopard single-deckers and, famously, Daimler Roadliner single-deckers. PMT was the first company to buy this rear-engined model, and built up the largest fleet, both buses and coaches. The Roadliner was not the happiest chassis and most of the PMT examples only had short lives. PMT's Daimler Fleetlines, in single-deck and double-deck form, were more successful. PMT's 1970 fleet totalled 500 buses (176 double-deck, 291 single-deck, 33 coaches) and included chassis by AEC, Albion, Daimler and Leyland, and bodies by Alexander, Burlingham, Duple, Marshall, Northern Counties, MCW, Plaxton and Willowbrook.

Since 1970 the ownership of bus operators in the West Midlands has changed greatly. West Midlands PTE absorbed the Coventry Corporation undertaking in 1974 and as Travel West Midlands is now the major operator in the National Express bus division. Of the other municipal operators, only Nottingham remains in local authority control; Burton's municipal buses are now run by Arriva; in 1974 East Staffordshire District Council

Left: A Wolverhampton Corporation Daimler Roadliner SRC6 with Strachans body wears WM fleetnames. The Roadliners were short-lived in the PTE fleet, as in so many fleets.
Geoff Lumb

Below: A few reminders of the liveries previously worn by the fleets that went into West Midlands PTE in 1969, starting with the glorious blue/cream of West Bromwich Corporation, here worn by a 1962 Daimler CVG6-30 with 74-seat Metro-Cammell bodywork, seen after the formation of the PTE.
Tony Moyes

Above: Walsall Corporation was famous for its distinctive vehicle policy. In the 1960s it bought a substantial fleet of these short-length Daimler Fleetlines with 6LW engines and Northern Counties 70-seat bodies complete with a short front overhang and an entrance behind the front axle. This is well shown in this 1968 photo at Stafford station.

Mark Page

Below: A more conventional Walsall Corporation Daimler, a 1961 CVG6-30 with 72-seat Metro-Cammell forward entrance body at Rugeley in 1966.

Mark Page

had taken over from Burton Corporation and in 1986 it merged with the growing independent operator, Stevensons.

PMT has had mixed fortunes over the years, but is now a FirstGroup company.

Midland Red's story since 1970 has seen the once-great empire reduced, then broken up. In 1973 over 400 buses and seven garages serving the West Midlands area were transferred to West Midlands PTE, although Midland Red partly offset this dramatic reduction in its influence by acquiring local independents like Cooper, Hoggins, Green Bus and Harper

Bros. Then in 1981 it was split into four bus companies – Midland Red (East) based in Leicester, Midland Red (North) based in Cannock, Midland Red (South) based in Rugby, and Midland Red (West) based in Worcester; there was also Midland Red Express, based at Digbeth, Birmingham, and Midland Red Omnibus Company, which continued an engineering function at the famous Central Works at Egbaston, Birmingham. Today the bus remnants of the company survive as parts of Arriva (East and North), First (West), and Stagecoach (South). ∎

Above: Birmingham City Transport favoured the locally-built Daimler Fleetline from the early 1960s and this chassis became the PTE standard into the 1970s. This is a 1965 Fleetline with Park Royal 72-seat body, at Station Street in 1968.

Mark Page

Left: Wolverhampton Corporation also favoured locally-built products, Guys in this case, and this is a 1963 Arab V with Park Royal 72-seat forward-entrance bodywork.

Geoff Lumb

Above: **For many years Midland Red designed and built the majority of the buses and coaches needed for its massive fleet. The D9 was its standard double-decker in the 1950s, and 350 were built between 1953 and 1957, all with Metro-Cammell bodies. This one is seen late in its life at Stafford.**
Mark Page

Left: **The BMMO D9 was built from 1958 until 1966 with advanced features like integral construction, independent front suspension and disc brakes. The distinctive front end design is seen in this 1967 photo of a 1961 delivery with BMMO 72-seat body.**
Mark Page

Above: While it was still producing its own D9 double-deckers, Midland Red started buying Alexander-bodied Daimler Fleetlines, known as the D12 type. This is a 1968 77-seater, showing signs of wintry conditions in this February 1969 photo at Gloucester bus station, working on the express service to Birmingham.
Edward Shirras

Opposite above: The S22 was another BMMO variant on the 36ft-long single-deck theme. This is a 1968 example with BMMO body.
Ian Allan Library

Right: A foretaste of things to come. In 1973 National Bus Company sold its Midland Red services in the West Midlands area to West Midlands PTE, resulting in the unusual sight of BMMO buses in PTE livery, like this 1963 D9 seen in Birmingham in the late 1970s.
T W Moore

The last new single-deck BMMO design was the S23, built from 1968 to 1970. This 1968 example with BMMO 51-seat body is seen at Banbury Cross in 1969.
Mark Page

Seen during its brief sojourn with Midland Red before sale to the
Isle of Man, a former Stratford Blue 1964 Leyland Titan PD3A/1
with 73-seat Willowbrook body.

T W Moore

Coventry's 1968 Fleetline deliveries were 18 CRG6LX with ECW
72-seat bodies.

T W Moore

An older BMMO-built single-decker, a 1964 S16 with 52-seat
BMMO body, at Leicester.
Tony Wilson

An interesting line-up at Stratford Blue's Warwick Road garage late in the company's separate existence. It shows, from the left, one of four 1963 Leyland Titan PD3/4 with Northern Counties 73-seat forward entrance bodies, one of the six Willowbrook-bodied 73-seat forward-entrance Titan PD3A/1 bought in 1963/64, and the 1970 Leyland Leopard PSUR1A/1 with Alexander Y type body. Although Stratford Blue had five Leyland Panthers on order when it was absorbed into Midland Red in 1971, but these were sold to Preston Corporation. The Titan PD3s went to Midland Red but were soon sold to Isle of Man Road Services.
Geoff Lumb

In the lighter red/cream livery adopted by Coventry Corporation in its final years, a 1963 Daimler CVG6 with Metro-Cammell Orion 63-seat body, among the last of many similar buses delivered to the undertaking.
Geoff Lumb

Although Coventry Corporation was an enthusiastic customer for Daimler chassis, produced in the same city, its first rear-engined buses were, to the surprise of many, 22 Leyland Atlanteans, PDR1/2 models with 76-seat Willowbrook bodies bought in 1964. They would remain unique and future deliveries would be of Daimler's equivalent Fleetline model.
Geoff Lumb

In 1969 Coventry received a further 18 Fleetlines, but with East Lancs 72-seat dual-door bodies, as seen in the city centre when new.
Edward Shirras

Above: Burton-upon-Trent Corporation standardised for many years on Guy Arabs with Gardner 5LW engines. Between 1963 and 1966 it bought 14 Daimler CCG5 with 61-seat Massey bodies. These had Guy-designed gearboxes and 5LW engines and so were similar to purchases from Guy.
Mark Page

Left: Burton turned to rear-engined single-deckers in 1969, following the delivery of its last Daimler CCG5s in 1968. These were three Daimler Fleetline SRG6LW with 44-seat Willowbrook bodies.
Geoff Lumb

Below: Typically BET fare for Potteries Motor Traction, a 1956 AEC Reliance MU3RV with 44-seat Weymann body at Hanley in 1971.
Mark Page

A famous bus in the PMT fleet was this Daimler with Northern Counties 69-seat forward entrance body. When new it was a CVD6-30 model with Daimler engine, but was re-engined by PMT with a Leyland O.600 unit, which makes it a CVL6-30. This impressive bus is seen at Hanley.
Tony Moyes

PMT had a famously mixed fleet and in the 1960s emerged as the main customer for Daimler's ill-fated Roadliner model. This is a late Roadliner, a 1969 SRP8 model with V8 Perkins engine, fitted with a 46-seat Plaxton body.
Geoff Lumb

Probably a more sensible Daimler purchase was the single-deck Fleetline, and this SRG6LX was one of 21 with Alexander W type bodies delivered in 1970.
Geoff Lumb

Above: On a drab day in Stoke, a PMT AEC Reliance 2MU3RV with
BET-design Alexander 45-seat body, one of 25 delivered in 1961
that were the company's only driver-only buses for many years.
Tony Moyes

Opposite above: At Mow Cop Castle in 1970 an early 36ft-long bus,
an AEC Reliance 2U3RA with Willowbrook 54-seat body, one of
109 delivered in 1962.
Tony Moyes

Right: Another of the short-lived Daimler Roadliners, a 1966 SRC6
(Cummins V6 engine) with 50-seat Plaxton body, at Chapel Chorlton.
Tony Moyes

In 1970 the independent, Harper Bros of Heath Hayes, Cannock, ran 30 buses and 28 coaches, including this 1968 Leyland Titan PD3A/1 with Northern Counties 72-seat body, seen here at Cannock. The company was acquired by Midland Red in 1974.
Mark Page

Green Bus of Rugeley, ran 41 buses and coaches on local services and was acquired by Midland Red in 1974. This former Halifax Corporation 1951 AEC Regent III with 56-seat Park Royal body is seen at Lichfield in 1969.
Mark Page

Stevenson of Uttoxeter grew from its roots in the 1920s and operated stage carriage routes between Uttoxeter and Burton-on-Trent and between Burton and Ashbourne. In 1970 it had 29 vehicles, mostly bought secondhand. It was destined to grow substantially in the 1980s and formed a significant part of what is now Arriva's presence in that area. This former Sheffield Corporation 1960 Leyland Leopard L1 with 44-seat Weymann body is seen at Uttoxeter in 1973.
Mark Page